12 Healthy Habits of Business Leadership

The Power of Investing in Yourself

Anna J. Campbell

ISBN: 1508542279
ISBN-13: 978-1508542278

DEDICATION

I have written this book for my daughter.

May she find purpose and happiness along the amazing and wondrous journey of her life.

Anna J. Campbell

ACKNOWLEDGMENTS

Mom and Dad, thank you for instilling in me the knowledge that anything is possible as long as I am open to believing in it and willing to work for it.

Brean, thank you for always believing in me and for encouraging me to challenge myself.

Jerdahn, thank you for reminding me that my happiness is not dependent on how other people see me or think of me, my happiness comes from within me.

Kari Campbell, thank you for helping me to stay motivated and for helping to edit many of the chapters of this book that just kept evolving!

Bobbie Asad, thank you for encouraging me to stick with it and never give up on finishing this project!

And I would like to thank all of the truly inspirational business leaders who have shared their insight, experiences, and accomplishments with me for this book. I would especially like to thank Beth Glover, Cindy Clark, Wendy VanHatten, Bobbie Asad, Jennifer Vaaler, Julie Bell Voorhees, Brenda Lagnese, Kim Draper, and Naomi Riley for taking the time to share their experiences with me. You have a true understanding of the many facets of business ownership, customer relationships, and appreciating life!

Thank you!

Anna J. Campbell

A NOTE TO THE READER

12 Healthy Habits of Business Leadership is filled with A-HA moments, joyful stumbling's, and triumphant acceptance of our humanity and true passion in life.

I always assumed that business success would mean wearing business suits, speaking in front of large audiences, receiving awards, and being acknowledged for my business savviness from every large business organization in the world.

Remembering that at our basic level we are drawn to be needed, productive, and useful. This has allowed me to stay focused on my true business success and personal happiness.

I hope that by reading *12 Healthy Habits of Business Leadership* you will be able to make your own business and life choices that will help bring you, your version of success and happiness.

Take comfort in knowing that just by giving yourself knowledge and understanding, you are already on your way!

Each chapter provides insight, related questions, related solutions, and an accountability chart.

"Invest in yourself and take a chance.
No one owes you the future you want.
You have to build it."
Unknown Author

CONTENTS

A NOTE TO THE READER..vii

Keep Your Head in the Game 1

   Keep Your Head in the Game: Questions................................. 3

   Keep Your Head in the Game: Solutions 7

   Business Accountability: Goals to accomplish this month................ 13

Expanding Your Skills 15

   Expanding Your Skills: Questions 18

   Expanding Your Skills: Solutions 21

   Business Accountability: Tracking Goals from last month 23

Attracting New Clients By Understanding Their Needs.......................... 25

   Attracting New Clients: Questions 29

   Attracting New Clients: Solutions 32

   Business Accountability: Tracking Goals from last month 34

Be A Super Star 36

   Be A Super Star: Questions 39

   Be A Super Star: Solutions 41

   Business Accountability: Tracking Goals from last month 43

Have A Thankful Heart.. 45

   Have a Thankful Heart: Questions 48

   Have a Thankful Heart: Solutions 50

   Business Accountability: Tracking Goals from last month 51

Stay Determined To Achieve Greatness 53

   Stay Determined To Achieve Greatness: Questions........................ 56

Stay Determined To Achieve Greatness: Solutions 57

Business Accountability: Tracking Goals from last month............... 58

Market Like a Ninja.. 60

Market Like A Ninja: Questions 66

Market Like A Ninja: Solutions 67

Business Accountability: Tracking Goals from last month............... 68

Delegating: The Art of Letting Go.. 70

Delegation: The Art of Letting Go: Questions 73

Delegation: The Art of Letting Go: Solutions................................. 74

Business Accountability: Tracking Goals from last month............... 75

Investing In Your Community 77

Investing In Your Community: Questions 80

Investing In Your Community: Solutions 82

Business Accountability: Tracking Goals from last month............... 84

Staying Sane By Forming a Power Group 86

Staying Sane: Questions... 88

Staying Sane: Solutions.. 90

Business Accountability: Tracking Goals from last month............... 91

Celebrating Your Successes 93

Celebrating Your Successes: Questions 96

Celebrating Your Successes: Solutions.. 97

Business Accountability: Tracking Goals from last month............... 98

Business Resources... 100

Business Plan Template... 105

References 108

Chapter 1

Keep Your Head in the Game

AS A BUSINESS OWNER, OUR TIME AND MONEY IS VERY
PRECIOUS. THE BETTER WE HANDLE OUR TIME AND
MONEY, THE MORE SUCCESSFUL OUR BUSINESS AND
OUR LIFE WILL BE.

When it comes time to invest in your business, be very careful
about how you invest, why you invest and where you invest.

How You Invest in Your Business

You will have many opportunities throughout your business career
to invest in your business. Not every opportunity will be the Right
opportunity. When faced with those opportunities, ask yourself
these questions.

- How is purchasing more product going to help your
  business success?

- How is purchasing more supplies going to help your
  business success?

1

- How is purchasing more lead generation tools going to help your business success?

- How is buying the next kit or sales pitch on google going to help your business success?

- Will this help save you time?

- Will this help you save or make more money?

Why You Invest in Your Business

Every day as a business leader you are faced with questions about how you will operate your business and how those decisions will affect your personal financial future and your business bottom line.

- Why is purchasing more ad space going to help your business success?

- Why is purchasing more product going to help your business success?

- Why is purchasing more odds and ends going to help your business success?

- Why is purchasing random books, magazines, guides, and event passes going to help your business success?

- Why are you investing your time?

- Why are you investing your money?

Staying focused will help you maintain a systematic rhythm during your work hours and your life.

Keep Your Head in the Game: Questions

Let's begin by writing down some thoughts:

There are no wrong answers here; this is very personal and open to your own specific business requirements and long-term plans.

Where will your Business be in 5 years?
- What will you be selling?
- Will you be running your own store, operating online or have your product in someone else's store?
- Will you have employees?

_____

_____

_____

_____

_____

_____

Where will your business be in 10 years?
- How much income will you be making?
- What will you be selling?
- How many employees will you have?
- Do you plan on selling your business?

_____

_____

_____

_____

_____

Now that you have written out your 5 and 10 year business plans, let's work on building a strong foundation for your business.

1. How much money do you need to start your business, pay your rent, pay your employees, purchase products, buy equipment, and everything else you need to start your business?

   _____

   _____

2. How much money do you have on hand to invest in your business during your first 3 years?

   _____

   _____

3. What are your options for financing? Business loan, personal savings, family loan, business investors?

   _____

   _____

4. Will you be working another job while starting this business?

   _____

   _____

5. Will you have health insurance while starting this business?

   _____

   _____

6. Are you creating your products, marketing your products, and selling your products to your clients by yourself?

_____

_____

7. If you hire employees, will you be offering paid vacations and health insurance to them?

_____

_____

8. Do you have a CPA? *It is wise to consult your CPA when starting a business so you understand what your obligations and expectations are from a tax liability standpoint. Your CPA might also have a more efficient book keeping system for you to use that might save you time and money in the long run.* Write down your CPA's name, address, and contact information:

_____

_____

9. Do you have an Attorney? Please ask your attorney to read through all contracts prior to signing them. *There may be hidden loop holes or requirements that you are not aware of, such as being responsible for repairing or completely replacing HVAC equipment, roofs, or completing interior infrastructure repairs.* Write down your Attorney's name, address, and contact information:

_____

_____

10. Have you filed the necessary paperwork?
    Not every business has the same requirements.

- ☐ City: business license, taxes
- ☐ County: business license, taxes
- ☐ State: sales tax, business name, type of business
- ☐ Federal Government: IRS, EIN (employee identification number)

Don't be discouraged.

This book is designed to help you learn how to build a strong business foundation. In order to do this, you need to understand the requirements of running a successful business, see the big picture, and be able to accomplish the small details to make this dream a reality.

Let's get to work on building your productive and profitable business!

Keep Your Head in the Game: Solutions

1. List each product or service, including its sales price:

Product   Price

_____

_____

_____

_____

_____

_____

_____

2. How much time does it take to build or provide each product/service?

Product   Time

_____

_____

_____

_____

_____

_____

_____

3. Are you able to teach someone else how to build or provide these products/services? Yes or No

- Are you willing to delegate this? Yes or No

4. Do you already have a client/customer list? Yes or No
How many clients/customers do you have? _____

Is your list organized and in one place? Yes or No

5. A. Let's talk about time. Check off the tasks below that relate to your business. Each one will take a different amount of time to accomplish. (Ignore the time column for now)

Time
- ☐ Communicating with clients (phone, email, in person) _____
- ☐ Packing products for shipping _____
- ☐ Delivering products to clients or post office _____
- ☐ Creating products or services _____
- ☐ Working with wholesale clients _____
- ☐ Working with retail clients _____
- ☐ Networking events/meetings _____
- ☐ Accounting/Bookkeeping _____
- ☐ Managing a shop or vendor space _____
- ☐ Creating a website _____
- ☐ Maintaining the website _____
- ☐ Creating marketing materials _____
- ☐ Delivering marketing materials _____
- ☐ Cold calling or meeting clients _____
- ☐ _____ _____
- ☐ _____ _____

5. B. Your available weekly hours not designated for day-to-day operations (unpaid work) are your remaining hours to work with clients. *Take a few minutes and go back through your list in 5A. Designate a specific amount of time required to complete each checked task, based on a weekly schedule.*

- • This number shows you how much time running your business takes each week. Delegating duties will help free up time that may give you more personal time.

6. Write down your work hours in ink (ink means commitment) on your paper or digital calendar for each day you plan to work during each week. Do this on a monthly basis. You will need to continue this until you know which hours are for work and which hours are for personal or family time.

Stop and designate your work hours on your calendar now.

7. Is product delivery required? Are client meetings required for your business? Will this add extra time or expenses? List everything:

_____

_____

_____

_____

8. Are there any restrictions on the type of product or service you want to provide in your current location or service area? You may need to check with your city, county, or state business offices to find out the specific restrictions for your area.

Yes or No

This could include zoning laws for serving alcohol. Some locations limit duplication of product or service types within a certain proximity to each other. Please investigate this, legally if necessary, before signing a lease.

If you find any restrictions, write them down here:

_____

_____

_____

9. What other companies already provide this product or service in your market area? Are they presently servicing your desired client base?

Write them down:

_____

_____

_____

10. What would be a good 3-5 word phrase that concisely embodies your business in a nutshell? This is called a tagline and is part of branding your business.

_____

11. Do you already have a logo? (A logo is an image that immediately communicates what your business is about.)

Yes   or   No

Describe it here: _____

12. What is your website URL? It should be as short as possible, easy to remember, and easy to spell:

_____

13. What is your business phone number? It should have a short and welcoming voice message:

_____

14. What is your email address? It should be short, easy to read, and easy to remember:

_____

Make sure your website URL, email address, and phone number are easily found and easy to read on your website, business cards, all social media accounts, and product packaging.

You are in business to retain new clients and make money. You are not a secret agent hoping clients will find you.

Attach a copy of your business license.

Business Accountability: Goals to accomplish this month.

Number of new clients to add to my existing client list: _____

Number of transactions/sales desired this month: _____

Number of networking events to attend this month: _____

Number of referrals to give others this month: _____

Number of marketing pieces to hand out or mail: _____

Check off the following as they are completed:

- ☐ Registered website domain. Date purchased: _____
- ☐ Updated client database
- ☐ Completed at least one update to website (blog post, product, etc.)
- ☐ Investigated competition
- ☐ Filed business paperwork
- ☐ Created a business tagline

Chapter 2

Expanding Your Skills

THE MOST EFFECTIVE WAY TO INVEST YOUR TIME AND MONEY IS IN <u>YOU</u>.

Building your understanding of how online and offline business strategies work, building your business branding and presence, and building a solid product or service line that you are passionate about is vital for your success. The better prepared You are, the more successful your Business will be.

I encourage you to attend at least one local educational workshop or class every few months and a regional or national business convention each year.

I believe that when we can walk away from an educational event with at least one nugget of new information and new business contacts, then it was worth it!

Throughout the years I have admired my friend and fellow business entrepreneur Cindy Clark with CC Transformational Coaching. She has shown me how valuable it is as business leaders to challenge myself and expose myself to new ideas and ways of understanding my business strategy and market.

I was speaking to Cindy Clark, a life and business coach, about my research for this book concerning education and training and she says, *"I'm a firm believer that when we continue to learn, upgrade our skills (or learn new ones), increase our knowledge or look for new paths, that we are preparing for the next level, whether it be in life or in business.*

Sometimes both. By expanding our knowledge, we continue to grow. Continue to move forward. Continue to evolve as human beings. Helping not only ourselves, but others as well. "

"Preparation meets opportunity" – the definition of luck.

"I continue to attend business workshops, webinars/teleseminars, conferences and conventions that are of interest to me and I know will help me, my business and my clients.

The most important thing I love about attending these events is all the wonderful people I may not otherwise meet. Looking to create and build a relationship is key.

I often try to meet the person holding the event and build a relationship with that person as well as the attendees. Building relationships and learning from these people, helps us to grow, strengthen ourselves and our businesses. "

Cindy Clark, Life and Business Coach
CC Transformational Coaching
Life and Business Coaching
Simple, Smart and Strategic Solutions for Savvy Women
Transform Your Life
www.cindywclark.com

Maybe you are not sure how you are going to get there, but I assure you, what is set in your heart and mind will happen. Once you focus on accomplishing your goals, nothing can stop you.

Maintaining a consistent training schedule is similar to a computer program having consistent updates or upgrades.

Upgrades provide improved virus software, new or improved options, etc. Just like this computer program, you and your business will need to update your skill set and level of understanding in order to remain competitive in the market place.

Spend some time thinking about how these educational events could benefit you and your business:

- Self-improvement
- Business ownership
- Skill enhancement
- Greater professional connections

I cannot emphasize enough the importance of your personal and business educational investment.

I can't guarantee your success if you do this, but I can guarantee your failure if you don't.

Expanding Your Skills: Questions

Stop and write down a list of different topics for educational workshops, classes, or conventions that you would be interested in attending or wish you had already attended:

_____

_____

_____

_____

Now that you have written out the topics of workshops, classes and conventions that you would like to attend, now it is time to do some research.

Don't groan or run away, you will thank me later for it.

1. What types of business organizations or groups are in your area? Chamber of Commerce, Rotary Clubs, Kiwanis Clubs, Women's Clubs, Men's Clubs, Charter organizations, networking groups, or community colleges? *Think of this as a treasure hunt.* Write down the ones you find:

_____

_____

_____

_____

2. Write down at least 3 areas within your business where you know you could use some help. Examples: budgeting, accounting, marketing, blogging, website maintenance, customer service, client retention techniques, marketing niche, etc.

_____

_____

_____

_____

3. From your group research in #1, what types of workshops, classes or conventions are any of them hosting for the upcoming year? Are any related to your personal interests or business focus? Would any of the topics help you with any weaknesses you have (ie: updating your website, understanding social media, learning how to network in person, creating a recognizable brand, etc.)?

Write these events down here:

_____

_____

_____

_____

_____

4. How much are they charging for their educational events? Plan to dedicate a minimum of $150 to $3,000 per year for training and networking opportunities. Keep this in mind as you start totaling up the costs; remember each one could have a tax benefit.

Check all costs including: main event fees, special food or banquet fees, any meals not included, hotel or parking fees.

_____

_____

_____

_____

_____

I am trying to get you to focus on educational workshops, classes, and conventions instead of just attending monthly general business meetings where you are less likely to receive new information, discover new business skills, or build longer lasting business relationships.

Expanding Your Skills: Solutions

1. Your first assignment in this chapter is to discover common ground. Ask around about the different networking or business groups in your area. Do any focus on your social interests or relate directly to your business? It is always helpful to be connected with like-minded people. Just visit a few groups until you find one that fits your needs.

By joining a group in your area, you will be building your circle of confidence. This group will support you when you have specific business questions or concerns. It will also provide you with a few people that you will learn to trust, and also feel comfortable referring business to. We will go into this further in chapter 10.

List out a few groups you will look into:

_____

_____

_____

_____

_____

2. Once you have chosen a group or two and have met a few of their members. Ask if any of them would be interested in attending a workshop, class or convention with you.

It is always easier and more fun to attend these events when there are other people to share it with.

3. The next step is to sign up for at least one upcoming workshop, class or convention.

Mark it on your calendar. Challenge yourself to do that today!

4. What do you need to accomplish before you attend? Plan to set aside extra funds for parking, lodging, food, and transportation.

_____

_____

_____

_____

_____

5. Before you network at the upcoming event, be sure to review your website and each of your marketing materials. ***Don't be caught without professional business cards.*** Up to date business cards are essential, scratching out is not allowed. That is very unprofessional.

Update everything with:
- ☐ current photo
- ☐ contact information (email, phone, website)
- ☐ services/products
- ☐ current pricing

6. And most importantly, **you must SHOW UP!** You must not allow anything to get in your way of attending this event. I know we talked about this before, but showing up is *crucial* to your success!

Business Accountability: Tracking Goals from last month

Number of new clients added to your database: _____

Number of transactions/sales closed: _____

Number of networking events attended: _____

Number of referrals given: _____

Number of marketing pieces delivered: _____

Goals to accomplish this month

Number of new clients to add to my client list: _____

Number of transactions/sales to complete: _____

Number of networking events to attend: _____

Number of referrals to give others: _____

Number of marketing pieces to hand out or mail: _____

Check off as you accomplish the following goals:

- ☐ Joined a group
- ☐ Signed-up for at least one educational event
- ☐ Updated my website
- ☐ Updated my business card
- ☐ Budgeted for Educational Expenses

Chapter 3

Attracting New Clients By Understanding Their Needs

ATTRACTING NEW CLIENTS WILL MAKE OR BREAK A
BUSINESS, EITHER NEW OR EXISTING.

*"Be somebody who makes everybody feel like somebody." Author
Unknown*

Two key elements you must be able to define:
- Who you want to work with
- What you want to provide them

I know this seems simple, but, in reality, your answers will help
you understand *where* to find new clients, *what* will attract new
clients, and *when* to take on new clients.

Take a few minutes to think about the people you like to spend your time with. How are they spending their personal and business time?

When you spend time with people during their "personal time" you are connecting with them on a much deeper and meaningful level. This is about building a relationship which will organically result in reaching your business goals.

When you connect with people during their "business time" you are able to determine the best way to market to them. This is about reaching a marketing goal.

Several business owners that I have worked with over the years have asked me how they can reach more customers without having a brick and mortar storefront. They felt that just having a website wasn't enough to attract clients in what they believed to be an over saturated market.

I have watched my friend Brenda Lagnese, owner of Furry Friends of Fuquay, grow her business into a booming and thriving income maker in a very short amount of time. Since she doesn't have a brick and mortar storefront and has still accomplished something that many other business owners are still trying to figure out, I asked her to share with us how she was able to reach her target market of clients and how she retained them.

Brenda says, "*I am the owner/pack leader of Furry Friends of Fuquay. I have been in business since July 2013 and have had tremendous success with my little company. Much of this success can be directly related to my initial eagerness to acquire good customers!*

In a service business, such as pet sitting, everyone knows that customers are the foundation of your success. Without them, you are no longer in business.

However, with the wrong ones, you could also be out of business, so you must be careful. So, how do you find customers?

At first, I tried advertising in the papers, but once I saw that it didn't work for such a local business, I switched up! I decided to spend $100 and stick paw prints and signs all over my little PT Cruiser convertible and make my car, my advertising base.

BAM, Furry Friends was on the map!!! I got customers everywhere I went: Wal-Mart, Kroger, or just to pick up my kids at school.

Seeing the social media craze, I started a Facebook page, so I can network with other local pet sitters and businesses. It's a great source for FREE advertising.

Local networking is where my business thrives!! I am a one-town girl and if you live in Fuquay, we are either friends or you have seen my crazy car and know my name. That way, when it's time for you to go on vacation, I am in your head to call.

Constantly seeing my car around town gives people the feeling that I'm the one to call when they need me. People want and love to spend their money on local businesses and I try to be that for Fuquay.

Just because I work out of my home doesn't mean I am not a local business. I am very active in my community where I live. I am involved with many charities and that also helps to get my business some free publicity. Getting involved where you live and work is KEY to your success.

I have an extensive background in the corporate world in sales and marketing and that was extremely useful when I went out on a crazy whim to "do my own thing". It taught me how to market my business without paying a lot out of pocket. We are in business to MAKE money, not waste it! Like the old saying goes, "work smarter, not harder".

In the past, I worked for a gift company and my job was to market to industry legends such as: Marshalls, Stein Mart and Wegmans. To get their attention, you MUST stand out from the rest. What can I do that 900 other small gift companies aren't doing??

That was the mental line I opened my business with. In my small, and amazing, town of Fuquay-Varina, there are tons of pet sitters to choose from. Why pick me?? I chose to keep my prices lower than the others and to exceed every one of my customers' expectations. I can up with specials like: chauffeured do park visits, which were an instant hit! Now I see them on almost all of my competitor's websites. People duplicate what works!

I send pictures, text messages and videos to the pets' owner to make them feel secure that their furry friends are safe, warm, and happy. I take their furry friends on car rides with the top down and they love it!!!

Just by coming up with some fun, new, and fresh ideas, you will capture that customer for life. Take care of your customers and they will take care of your business!

Once a customer is acquired, it should be easy to keep them. In a service business, they will be the ones working for you to acquire new clients. Do a great job for them and they will recommend you to their neighbors, friends, and family.

This also holds true if you do a bad job, so be careful. One bad apple can spoil the bunch!! Do the BEST job you can for them and NEVER take them for granted. They are the reason you are enjoying your success, so always keep a grateful heart and don't forget to say, "Thank you".

Brenda Lagnese
Furry Friends of Fuquay
www.furryfriendsoffuquay.com
www.facebook.com/furryfriendsoffuquay
(919) 760-5824

Attracting New Clients: Questions

What activities or hobbies do your customers enjoy? Where do they like to shop? How do they prefer to purchase products or services similar to yours (online, in store, by catalog)?

Go ahead and write down all the ideas that pop into your head. You might even ask your friends and family these questions.

_____

_____

_____

_____

1. Do you enjoy the same activities as your clients, such as attending walking groups or taking road trips? Do you both have pets? Do you frequent the same parties or events? Understanding that individual clients tend to fall into group categories is ideal for marketing campaigns.

Please just remember that each client must remain unique even though you may be meeting them in a group setting or corresponding with them through a group marketing campaign.

(If this is unclear, please visit my website or contact me for further clarification.)

Take a few minutes and write down different activities you and your clients both enjoy or appreciate:

_____

_____

_____

Break your clients up into groups of similar interests:
Client Group (A – D)   List your common interest (dogs, walking, etc.)

Group A

_____

Group B

_____

Group C

_____

Group D

_____

2. What is going on in the world around you? How is the economy in your local area or customer area? What is the unemployment rate? All of these relate to your customers ability to purchase your product/service.

_____

_____

3. Is your product/service a need or a want for your desired client base? _____

4. In order to determine your clients' needs you need to ask them. By understanding your current client's needs, you will better understand what to offer in order to attract new clients.

A fun and easy way to ask your clients is by creating a short email or printed Survey. Start by just asking 2-3 questions. Most clients love giving feedback about your current type of services or products, your business hours, parking issues, pricing, or what items they would love for you to offer.

Survey Monkey, an online survey program, provides a free and easy way to get started with your next customer survey. https://www.surveymonkey.com Other business resources can be found in chapter 12.

Write down some questions you will include in your survey:

_____

_____

_____

_____

5. What is the age of your target market? Are they getting older?

_____

6. Are you customers' needs different now than they were five or ten years ago? Are they married, divorced, having children, empty nesters?

List how they are different:

_____

_____

_____

_____

7. Are your customers now purchasing more for their children, grandchildren or themselves?

_____

8. Does your target market have a higher or lower income than before? _____

Attracting New Clients: Solutions

Focusing on what your consumer is looking for, what they are needing, and how much they have to spend will help you know what you need to fill your store with, how to market your business, and how they are going to find you.

Learning about your current customers is critical to understanding how you will attract new customers.

1. Ask your customers how they found you.

_____

_____

_____

2. Ask your friends how they find similar products or services when they are buying.

_____

_____

_____

3. Ask your family who they are most often purchasing your type of product or service for (themselves, children, etc.).

_____

_____

_____

4. Ask business associates who are selling similar items how their sales are doing, over the past 6-12 months.

_____

_____

_____

5. Staying in tune with your local market and the market around your specific product/service is crucial for how your business will survive long-term.

6. How many new clients would you like to have this year? _____

7. Divide your answer to question # 6 by 12: _____

This is the number of clients you wish to attract each month. Now, we have a number to work towards! Let's stay focused and start building that client list!

Business Accountability: Tracking Goals from last month

Number of new clients added to your database: _____

Number of transactions/sales closed: _____

Number of networking events attended: _____

Number of referrals given: _____

Number of marketing pieces delivered: _____

Goals to accomplish this month

Number of new clients to add to my client list: _____

Number of transactions/sales to complete: _____

Number of networking events to attend: _____

Number of referrals to give others: _____

Number of marketing pieces to hand out or mail: _____

Chapter 4

Be A
Super Star

"Don't confuse Leadership with Status." Lolly Daskal

As two well-known characters from a fairy tale of German origin, recorded by the Brothers Grimm, Hansel and Gretel insured their freedom by leaving bread crumbs for their father to find them. If we consider our business in this same way, we should be leaving physical and virtual bread crumbs everywhere leading our potential clients back to our website or storefront.

Your business presence may include a physical location, website, business Facebook page, Twitter account, Instagram account, LinkedIn account, billboards, magazine ads, newsletters, virtual and/or printed marketing materials.

Packaging sells products and helps gift recipients know where to buy more. Businesses with products should make sure to promote their brand (logo, business name, tag line, address, website URL, phone number) on all of the items sold to customers. Your brand should also be visible on all packaging (boxes, bags), flyers, business cards, brochures, catalogs, and of course on your website and all social media.

For businesses that depend on local clientele, you may also be listed with the local chamber of commerce, local or national charities/organizations you support, and participate in or sponsor local events that directly relate to your business.

For businesses operated completely online you should make sure your online presence is easy to read, filled with information, products/services, and ways for customers to easily get in touch with you.

During this chapter we will make sure that your business can be found by the people you want to serve and continue to provide inspiration to those you are already building a relationship with.

While visiting Topsail Island I noticed a prominent billboard advertising a local business, the bumblebee Market. The advertising was easy to read with bright colors and had the feeling of elegance and fun. I just had to visit this gift shop while I was there.

When I did stop by I was welcomed and encouraged to take my time and enjoy browsing through their delicious chocolates, fun household decoration items, comfortable clothing, and so much more.

Julie Bell Voorhees is the owner of The Bumblebee Market which is a truly magical gift shop. Her business doesn't have the ideal location for being physically near her customers throughout the year; however her business does have the wonderful opportunity of constantly attracting new clients who are visiting the island.

Not only does Julie prominently advertise her business on the island, she even gives you reasons to keep going back during your stay by organizing fun Ladies Night shopping events where you can purchase beautiful gifts at amazing discounts! She also encourages you to stay in touch and continue receiving savings throughout the year through her website and business Facebook page while you are away from the island.

Before leaving the island I made sure to sign-up for Julie's newsletter and followed her Facebook page. I was so impressed with how well Julie stayed in touch with me and how she still brought her sunshine into my day with her posts and emails.

 I asked Julie how much of an impact her online presence had for maintaining current customers and attracting new ones. Julie says, *"For me, social media and our general online presence wasn't started to meet new customers, it was created to stay in touch with all the great people I have the pleasure to meet throughout the year.*

I can think of so many families that started coming when their children were little, and now they are all taller than me (not hard to accomplish, but still...). Spouses that have come in to tell us that their loved one passed away and loved coming to the store and they just wanted to share it with us.

It was terrible to think we'd have to wait another year to be in contact with them. Most of them take the time to tell us that our emails and social media make them feel like they are here, on the island, on vacation and enjoying themselves.

So I come from that perspective.... the one that extends who we are in person, to online. It's a fun benefit that we get to meet even more great people! It's not the way other businesses look at it, but it works for us!"

Julie Bell Voorhees
Bumblebee Market
http://www.shopthebee.com/
513 Roland Avenue in Surf City,
North Carolina 28445
Topsail Island

Be A Super Star: Questions

One of the easiest ways to learn about your current business market is researching similar businesses that are already successful and have a presence online or in your community.

Take a few minutes and think about some businesses you know that are similar to yours, others that compliment your products or services, and fellow business owners that you would happily refer business to.

Write down the names of the businesses that come to mind:

Businesses who are Similar to mine:

_____

_____

_____

Business who are not the same but Complimentary to mine:

_____

_____

_____

Businesses I find Referral Worthy:

_____

_____

_____

1. What is your website URL?
   www._____

2. When was the last time you updated your website with current products/services, contact information, and pictures? _____

3. What is your business Facebook page URL?

www._____

4. What is your Pinterest account URL?

www._____

5. What is your twitter account URL?

www._____

6. What is your LinkedIn URL?

www._____

7. Do you have current brochures, catalogs or flyers for your business?

8. Do you print them as you need them, or do you have use a printer to print them in bulk?

9. Do you have signage that is easy to see from the road if you have a brick and mortar business?

10. Do you have a website that is easy to find if you do business strictly online?

11. Do you have an easy to see and visible "Open" sign for a brick and mortar business?

12. Is it easy for website visitors to find your Contact Form, phone number or email address on your website?

Be A Super Star: Solutions

1. Making sure your business is in front of the most people as possible will help keep your business in their mind when they are ready to purchase your service or product.

2. Your business presence must be current and provide a very specific need or want. Always focus your message to be filling that specific need or want.

3. The reason why having a website for all types of businesses (even if you do business by referral only) is to provide a source for references and feedback for current and past clients. This is a public way of thanking past clients, showing past products/services, and by providing a place to support your chosen charities/organizations.

4. Depending on your type of business, your website should be updated at least twice a year. Remember that search engines love fresh content on your website.

5. Having a business Facebook page is not for you, but for your clients that use Facebook. It gives them the opportunity to like and share your posts with their friends/family that they believe would benefit from your product/service.

Do not post more than 3 things a day on your Facebook business page. If you blog, you can have your blog/website set-up to automatically send an update to your Facebook page about the blog post you have written.

Do not post any personal photos or personal posts about where you are eating or what your family is doing on vacation to your business Facebook page.

6. Pinterest is a great way to share pictures and organize ideas for projects by using pictures instead of words.   If you blog, you can "pin" the photos you use in your blog post onto your related Pinterest "boards".

7. Twitter can be used as an active communication tool with fellow business owners or clients. It can also be used as an automatic feed of communication from your website.

8. LinkedIn is your Professional profile online. Everyone who is in business or wishes to be employed needs to have a current LinkedIn profile account. This is an easy way for many businesses and individuals wishing to do business with you, to see if you are a real person and what your past accomplishments and endeavors have been. A LinkedIn profile provides creditability.

9. Flyers should be included with every purchase. They should include basic information about your business, phone number, email address and website URL. The purpose of the flyer is to highlight a current sale, upcoming event you are participating in or a charity/organization you support (Such as a school you support with their sports calendar, etc.).

Maintaining an easy to find business in person or online is critical for a new business or one dependent on new clients to maintain a strong stream of income.

Business Accountability: Tracking Goals from last month

Number of new clients added to your database: _____

Number of transactions/sales closed: _____

Number of networking events attended: _____

Number of referrals given: _____

Number of marketing pieces delivered: _____

Goals to accomplish this month

Number of new clients to add to my client list: _____

Number of transactions/sales to complete: _____

Number of networking events to attend: _____

Number of referrals to give others: _____

Number of marketing pieces to hand out or mail: _____

Chapter 5

Have A Thankful Heart

THIS IS A WONDERFUL TIME TO THANK YOUR CLIENTS, FRIENDS AND FAMILY FOR THEIR SUPPORT, ENCOURAGEMENT AND LOYALTY.

"One kind word can change someone's entire day."
Author Unknown

We all have those special people in our lives that have listened to us, made suggestions when we were lost, or just cared enough to drop by when we weren't sure about how things were going.

JJ Ramberg shares 183 essential tips that will transform your small business in her book, *It's Your Business*. Three of the most poignant topics she covers in her book include: End customer interactions on a positive note, Respond to negative customer feedback positively, Partner with people who reach a similar audience.

One of the most awkward situations for a business leader is responding to negative feedback. I cringe every time I see someone slam the customer, respond with hate, or completely disregard the person's comments.

Always be courteous when someone leaves a review or comment. It is often harder for a customer to leave a bad review than to just never let you know. As a business leader you need to know all the good and bad about your business. Otherwise, you will never be able to correct issues that could potentially close your doors.

Showing gratitude isn't always about thanking someone for something nice they did, sometimes it is about thanking people for taking the time to help you be a better business owner, business leader, or provide a better product or service.

Beth Glover, owner of Merle Norman Spa & Boutique in Fuquay-Varina, regularly posts thankful and praising quotes on her social media sites about other local businesses. She is always reminding everyone how thankful she is for her customers and for the supportive business community she works in. I admire her consistent approach for sharing joyful praise about fellow business owner's accomplishments instead of just focusing on her own business triumphs.

I asked Beth why it was so important to her to share praise for other businesses on her business social media sites instead of just focusing on her own business. Beth says, *"As part of a small business community it is important for all of us to succeed. The more people that visit the area, the more opportunities arise for customers to be exposed to a unique shopping experience at each of the individually owned stores.*

As I have had the opportunity to get to know many of the local business owners and appreciate what they bring to the community, I am proud to promote their business and not compete with them.

Together we can be more successful and create a shopping experience where the customers will continue to visit, which is a benefit for all the businesses in the area and it also promotes our thriving downtown business community."

Beth Glover
Merle Norman Spa & Boutique
208 S. Main St., Fuquay-Varina, NC 27526
www.merlenormanstudio.com/mn-10013
www.facebook.com/merlenorman.fuquayvarina
(919) 552-3751

The most powerful control you have in your business success is how you respond to positive and negative feedback.

From experience, I learned that by responding with understanding and sincere appreciation to a customer's complaint, I not only earned their continued business, but she was so grateful that I accepted her complaint, and I dealt with it in a mature and helpful way, she told all of her friends and family about me and I gained many new long-term customers through her.

Have a Thankful Heart: Questions

1. Take a few minutes and write down some of your favorite business owners who have shared advice and time with you:

_____

_____

_____

_____

2. Take a few minutes and write down the names of your clients, friends, and family that you have not spoken to or heard from within the past few weeks, months or years:

_____

_____

_____

_____

3. Every month you should have a goal of how many people you are going to reach out to. A few ways to stay in contact with people on your list are: mailing a card, dropping off a little "thinking of you" note and gift, calling them on the phone, or meeting them for lunch or coffee. It is not appropriate to use a newsletter or email for thanking your clients.

Write down each way you will use to contact your clients:

_____

_____

_____

4. When was the last time you reached out to your clients with a mailed card, nice phone call, drop by (spur of the moment visit), or by sending them a gift? (Date and name client(s):

_____

_____

_____

_____

5. When you did reach out to your clients, which method worked the best? How much time did it take for you to see results? Results can be: receiving a referral, clients make a new purchase, client phones or drops in for a visit.

_____

_____

6. How much did it or will it cost you to reach out to your clients. Costs could be in purchasing notecards and stamps, small gifts, or nothing if you dropped by or called just to say hi.

Costs incurred:

_____

7. How do you keep track of your clients? Do you have them saved in an excel spreadsheet, online client management software, or written down in an address book?

_____

8. How often do you update this list? Occasionally or as new clients are secured? _____

Have a Thankful Heart: Solutions

1. Running a business is a very time intensive endeavor. However, maintaining a healthy client database will be how you truly keep your business successful.

2. A healthy client database needs several things to grow:

- Stay in regular contact with your clients. This could be sending out a monthly newsletter online or paper, seeing them around town, attending similar networking meetings or charity events.

- Keep up to date on what is happening in your client's lives: new babies, moving, life changes, birthdays, etc.

3. The care and attention you give to your best clients reminds them of how important they are to you and that you truly appreciate them.

Business Accountability: Tracking Goals from last month

Number of new clients added to your database: _____

Number of transactions/sales closed: _____

Number of networking events attended: _____

Number of referrals given: _____

Number of marketing pieces delivered: _____

Goals to accomplish this month

Number of new clients to add to my client list: _____

Number of transactions/sales to complete: _____

Number of networking events to attend: _____

Number of referrals to give others: _____

Number of marketing pieces to hand out or mail: _____

Chapter 6

Stay Determined To Achieve Greatness

FINDING BUSINESS PURPOSE FOR YOURSELF OFTEN STEMS BACK TO HOW YOU LEARNED THE VALUE OF PURPOSE FROM YOUR FAMILY, TEACHERS, AND EMPLOYERS.

"You must make a Choice to take a Chance or your life will never Change." **Kim Garst**

Purpose is a lofty reason why you are trying to accomplish something. Merriam-Webster defines *purpose* as, "the feeling of being determined to do or achieve something".

I have found that it is easier for me to understand my *business purpose* while sharing past experiences, thoughts, or ideas with a fellow business woman. She can often put all of my little "purpose" experiences together into a larger picture, and then share with me her larger view of what my *business purpose* may be from her perspective.

If you are not able to discover your *business purpose* on your own, find someone you trust and share with them information you believe will be helpful for you both to potentially discover your *business purpose* together. We will go into more detail about Forming Your Power Group in chapter 10.

I absolutely love *The Happiness Project* by Gretchen Rubin. This isn't necessarily a business related book, but it is one that would help everyone who is a business leader! One of the most important sections of her book that I believe truly affects all leaders is *Enjoy Now*.

We are so often focused on next week's sale, next month's quota, and next year's budget that we often fail to appreciate Now.

You can only truly be happy if you can *Enjoy Now*. Gretchen mentions, "The arrival fallacy is a fallacy because, though you may anticipate great happiness in arrival, arriving rarely makes you as happy as you anticipate".

She reminds us that the ever looking forward doesn't provide us with the full enjoyment of now. Appreciating where you are, right now, right here. That is the key to accepting your happiness, now.

Sure, tomorrow your happiness could grow, or lessen... but for today, accept your happiness and relish in it! Appreciate everything good happening in your life and your business at this very moment.

Your business purpose is what brings you the happiness to continue opening your store, continue creating your products, and continue communicating with your clients.

Stay Determined To Achieve Greatness: Questions

1. Who is benefitting from your business? Is it you, your family, someone in the community, a group of people, animals?

_____

_____

2. How are they benefitting from your business? Is it financial support paying for school, paying your mortgage, exposure for their cause, raising awareness about public issues?

_____

_____

3. Do you feel driven by this purpose?

4. Are you motivated to run your business each day with joy and happiness?

5. Are you excited about why you are running your business or is it dragging you down?

6. Would you like to dig deeper and understand what your true purpose is?

Stay Determined To Achieve Greatness: Solutions

1. Figuring out who is benefitting from your business will help you also understand why you are running your business. And if you figure out, it isn't who you want to be benefitting from your business, then changes need to be made.

2. Your business should be serving the purpose you have in mind. Whether that is paying your mortgage, bringing in a second stream of income, paying for student debt, or just providing some extra spending money.

3. Understanding how the beneficiary of your business is benefitting, will help you make this stronger or change it to be benefitting the right person.

4. If you are not being driven by your current business purpose, then you may soon become bored, lose focus, or become aggravated and resentful. Being driven by your business purpose is one of the strongest motivators you have.

Business Accountability: Tracking Goals from last month

Number of new clients added to your database: _____

Number of transactions/sales closed: _____

Number of networking events attended: _____

Number of referrals given: _____

Number of marketing pieces delivered: _____

Goals to accomplish this month

Number of new clients to add to my client list: _____

Number of transactions/sales to complete: _____

Number of networking events to attend: _____

Number of referrals to give others: _____

Number of marketing pieces to hand out or mail: _____

Chapter 7

Market Like a Ninja

UTILIZING THE EXISTING MARKETING IN YOUR AREA IS IDEAL FOR YOUR INDIVIDUAL SALES DURING ANY TIME OF YEAR.

"There comes a moment when you have to stop revving up the car and shove it into gear." David Mahoney

You may cross-market with two or three other businesses with a joint marketing plan that allows you to reach more customers at a lower overall marketing cost.

While researching business marketing trends and insights, I found *The Martha Rules:* 10 essentials for achieving success as you start, build, or manage a business written by Martha Stewart.

Martha shares insight into several basic areas of business such as, Appeal to your customers' wants and needs, Beware the echo chamber: assembling an advisory board, and Take risks not chances.

The first two are fairly understandable and make complete sense. The third tidbit really made me start thinking.

Martha says that, "*In business, there's a difference between a risk and a chance. A well-calculated risk may very well end up as an investment in your business. A careless chance can cause it to crumble. And when an opportunity presents itself, never assume it will be your last.*"

This really hit home for me because I often jump at marketing opportunities without taking any amount of time to research them, consider other options, or understand the consequences. While this habit hasn't always hurt me, it hasn't always provided me with the best results either. I now understand that it is ok to be brave and take a risk, but it should be a well informed and calculated risk.

Understanding how to reach the most people within your target market using the least amount of time and money will grow your bottom line and shrink your expenses.

I asked a local gift shop owner, Bobbie Asad with Mad Hatter in downtown Fuquay-Varina, what she thought was the most important reason for marketing her business and she says, "*By raising awareness of my business, the brand and products through marketing, I have built a larger audience of current and potential customers.*

Marketing campaigns may not always bring people to my door immediately, sometimes months after the campaign they will stop in and mention seeing my ad.

I believe the most important facet of marketing is focusing on my target market. My ultimate goal is to bring customers in the door and then create repeat business.

Personally, I believe if you are not marketing your business, you are not moving forward.

My marketing strategy is always to inform people about Mad Hatter's existence and products. I have used direct mail, newspaper ads, press releases, Facebook and Twitter.

You must get the word out about your business whether thru print media or online. Try them all; see what works best for your business. Each of these avenues reaches a different audience."

Bobbie Asad
Mad Hatter in Fuquay-Varina
107 South Main Street,
Fuquay-Varina, NC 27526
http://madhatternc-com.webs.com
https://www.facebook.com/madhatter9251
(919) 557-5771

Bobbie has created a vibrant gift store with a high quality selection of teas, condiments, exquisite hats, and accessories. Her storefront has only been open for a year and yet she already has a strong following that drives in from all over the state and her business reach has been expanding to new customers in Virginia and throughout the country.

Often times a well-timed phone call, email, or personal note just thanking customers for supporting your business is an easy and effective way for existing customers to recommit to using your product or service.

How Business Branding Increases Sales

The contemporary definition of Brand according to dictionary.com is: in marketing, the use of logos, symbols, or product design to promote consumer awareness of goods or services. Examples: Branding has made companies like Apple successful.

While this word isn't new, we still seem to have a difficult time understanding the concept and purpose of branding.

Ekaterina Walter a writing contributor for Forbes says, *"… my advice is to go way back, to look deeper, and to ask yourself some fundamental questions about what your brand stands for and what its purpose is. Because unless you are very clear on the answers to those questions, you will not only be unable to create a strong brand, but to communicate your brand to others as well."*

Following along the same lines, Liz Papagni a contributing author with Business 2 Community says, *"A well-branded organization has the ability to be recognized, earn loyalty, and define themselves within their market. However, your efforts to brand your organization won't get far if they're not authentic."*

Lou Ibriano, CEO, TrinityOne, Inc. a contributing author for American Express really helps us focus as he says, *"The adjectives and characteristics that make up your brand should differentiate you from your competitors and provide a clear understanding of what your business is not only capable of doing, but also what it is known for."*

Heidi Cohen with Actionable Marketing Guide reminds us that, *"Branding should be incorporated into every interaction you have across owned, social media and third party platforms as well as in real life."*

Alyssa Mattero a contributing author with Shareaholic explains, *"Branding is about conditioning your target audience to associate your company with a response, specifically something impactful and relevant that speaks to their needs or concerns."*

According to Sara Germano and Anna Prior in their article published in the Wall Street Journal, *"Over the years, Under Armour has built up its footwear offerings and expanded its fleet of concept stores, targeting new international markets for a brand best known in the U.S. as a vendor of performance athletic apparel.*

The result is that Under Armour is gaining strength in international and footwear sales, better positioning it to be a competitor to bigger rivals like Nike Inc. and Adidas AG ."

Creating a solid brand with effective reference to your product or service and maintaining a strong business presence in the market place will help to increase your sales!

Annual Marketing Calendar

Create a basic marketing calendar and add to it throughout the year. Every month should include one newsletter printed or emailed, individual blog posts for each major topic covered in your newsletter, and feeds sent out to your LinkedIn, Twitter, and Facebook accounts.

Your marketing calendar is a great place to jot down annual events that attract new clients and remind existing clients it is time to shop.

How Can Your Customers Help With Marketing?

Beth Glover, owner of Merle Norman Spa & Boutique in Fuquay-Varina, is in a unique position where her business helps her clients feel and look their best. I asked Beth to share with us how this may be an excellent way for her clients to be marketing her business for her.

Beth says, *"Our customers are our business, the best way for us to obtain new customers is through word of mouth. Our customers are our walking billboards. When they are confident and feel good about themselves due to the way Merle Norman skin care and cosmetics makes them look and how the clothing makes them feel, they become our best possible way of reaching new clients.*

When someone receives a compliment on their look, skin or clothes they have purchased from us, they are going to let other people know where they purchased these items and how they were treated.

We strive to create a personal relationship with our customers and provide them with the best experience possible."

Beth Glover
Merle Norman Spa & Boutique
208 S. Main St., Fuquay-Varina, NC 27526
www.merlenormanstudio.com/mn-10013
www.facebook.com/merlenorman.fuquayvarina
(919) 552-3751

This feedback is excellent advice for any service related business that provides clients with products or services to improve their physical appearance or wellbeing.

Market Like A Ninja: Questions

1. What services or products do you have that could capture the meaning or purpose of each specific town event, local school event or community holiday? (Such as hats and teas for a community garden party event)

_____

_____

2. Who is your target market? Who would be interested in receiving your product or service and why would they be purchasing it?

_____

_____

3. How will you share information about your new products or services to current and new clients? (Flyers, banners, emails, balloons, signage, newsletters, postcards, notecards, billboards, magazine ads, social media, website)

_____

_____

_____

There is no better time to start marketing your business than Today!

Market Like A Ninja: Solutions

1. Prepare an overall marketing campaign for your business.

2. Prepare a marketing campaign for each of your key product or service lines.

3. Prepare a marketing campaign for projects your business works with other business partners or organizations with.

4. Share information about charities or causes you and your employees support.

5. Remember to use high resolution photographs or images with all of your marketing. Print marketing should include images with 300 DPI (dots per inch) or higher.

Business Accountability: Tracking Goals from last month

Number of new clients added to your database: _____

Number of transactions/sales closed: _____

Number of networking events attended: _____

Number of referrals given: _____

Number of marketing pieces delivered: _____

Goals to accomplish this month

Number of new clients to add to my client list: _____

Number of transactions/sales to complete: _____

Number of networking events to attend: _____

Number of referrals to give others: _____

Number of marketing pieces to hand out or mail: _____

Chapter 8

Delegating: The Art of Letting Go

"Surround yourself with the best people you can find, delegate authority, and don't interfere as long as the policy you've decided upon is being carried out." **Ronald Reagan**

To help you remain focused on the important aspects of your business and not get lost in the hustle and bustle of everything going on in your business it is wise to delegate duties to responsible individuals and outside businesses that can help alleviate you of duties that will not help you bring in a large Return On your Investment (ROI).

Outsourcing mundane or repetitive tasks such as creating a monthly newsletter, updating your website blog, writing and posting press releases to online social media and offline media sources can provide you with the necessary time to network in person with potential buyers, attend events to purchase products for your store, and to conduct more business that will have a higher ROI.

When you have an organized life, you can work on having an organized business. We do not simply become a different person when we change our mindset from personal life to business. As a business leader, we are still the same core person at all times.

As you delegate time consuming duties to responsible parties, you will be freeing up valuable time as the leader of your business to manage and direct the productivity and financial flow your business needs to be successful.

One of my favorite parts of the book *womenomics* written by Claire Shipman and Katty Kay is the simple revelation they share under the *womenomics Balance Sheet*.

Cost 1: *"Isn't a pay cut of any sort a big step backward?"*

"Don't think hourly rate – think value, as Jennifer discovered. Even if you have to make financial cutbacks, the value to your life of gaining a few extra hours each week is potentially huge. It can make the difference between sanity and chaos."

Many of my friends and clients tell me that this is often one of the biggest reasons they have decided to start their own business. They want more freedom. They want more time with their family. They want the control of when, how, why, and where.

Unfortunately, many of us forget that this was our main reason, as we often change our focus and all of our "time" into trying to make more money.

Many times we see "delegating" as costing us money. Instead, "delegating" actually frees us up to produce more money in a much shorter and less stressful amount of time.

By delegating away small non-income producing business responsibilities, we free ourselves up to tackle all of the income producing opportunities!

Delegation: The Art of Letting Go: Questions

1. How much time does it take for you to create your monthly newsletter?

_____

2. How much time does it take to sit in your shop "waiting" for new clients to show up?

_____

3. How much time does it take for you to make your products?

_____

4. How much time does it take for you to maintain your client database?

_____

5. How much time does it take for you to:
   - Update website
   - Create blog posts
   - Creating marketing materials
   - Emailing or handing out marketing materials

_____

6. How much times does it take for you to complete your monthly bookkeeping?

_____

7. How much time does it take for you to mail or deliver orders?

_____

Delegation: The Art of Letting Go: Solutions

1. Hiring someone who already possesses the necessary skills will save you possible time, money and stress in the long run.

2. Hiring an experienced bookkeeper will save you time from learning the available accounting software, the time of inputting and correctly calculating all of the figures and from having the necessary understanding of preparing your taxes, annual or quarterly sales tax receipts and other necessary accounting needs for your specific business.

3. Hiring an experienced marketing specialist or an advertising firm will save you money from purchasing expensive graphic programs, time for learning the programs, and understanding presentation and how to appeal to your target market.

4. If you are not good at creating pleasing packaging presentations for your clients, it may behoove you to hire someone else to package your products for gift baskets that are being sold, used in photographs or being donated. Your product packaging needs to provide the best possible first impression it can.

5. For service industries you may have client files and information that needs proper documentation and organization. Hiring someone else who already possesses this skill set will save you time and money in the long run.

Business Accountability: Tracking Goals from last month

Number of new clients added to your database: _____

Number of transactions/sales closed: _____

Number of networking events attended: _____

Number of referrals given: _____

Number of marketing pieces delivered: _____

Goals to accomplish this month

Number of new clients to add to my client list: _____

Number of transactions/sales to complete: _____

Number of networking events to attend: _____

Number of referrals to give others: _____

Number of marketing pieces to hand out or mail: _____

Chapter 9

Investing In Your Community

GROWING YOUR BUSINESS TAKES TIME AND COMPASSION.

"Walk with the dreamers, the believers, the courageous, the cheerful, the planners, the doers, the successful people with their heads in the clouds and their feet on the ground. Let their spirit ignite a fire within you to leave this world better than when you found it." Author Unkown

Being a successful business leader requires the drive to maintain a schedule, the energy to keep up with your competition, and the "get-it-done" attitude to succeed.

As business leaders we can often feel overwhelmed and all alone. The truth is that we are never truly alone. We are surrounded by a community of fellow business leaders, clients, friends, and neighbors. Whether your community is online or offline, they are your community.

Investing a specific and focused amount of time, energy and finances in one's community often helps the contributing businesses to grow and flourish.

Dictionary.com defines Community as: 1. Social group of any size whose members reside in a specific locality, share government, and often have a common cultural and historical heritage. 2. a locality inhabited by such a group. 3. a social, religious, occupational, or other group sharing common characteristics or interest and perceived or perceiving itself as distinct in some respect from the larger society which it exists (usually preceded by the): the business community; the community of scholars.

Wendy VanHatten has been an entrepreneur for as long as I have known her. She is a well-established magazine editor, published author, and she is always telling me how great her local, national, and global community is! I knew she would be able to share some very clear and helpful insight into why it is so important for us to invest in our community.

"Investing, to me, is engaging in the community. While this sounds ambiguous, the great thing about engaging in your community is that you can tailor it to you and to the community you live in. Perhaps you do need to invest more money locally or spend more time locally. Or, perhaps it's as simple as finding out what your community needs are and going from there.

For me, investing in my community means a variety of things I can do personally. As a travel writer, it means I have the opportunity to showcase my community. When I write an article about yearly festivals, local wineries, or the newest bistro in town...I'm helping promote our local businesses to the world. To do this, I develop a good rapport with business owners to help me understand their business and how they fit into the community. When people ask me what to visit when they come to this area, I have a better understanding of events and businesses. Publications like personal touch articles and ask me to write more, giving more opportunities to promote my community.

As a magazine editor, I also have the opportunity to visit with local businesses to see what their needs are and when I can help. Sometimes it's as simple as offering a small article on the latest trend in our community. Do we have a current fundraiser for a local child in need? Do we have an upcoming event that will support a fantastic, community wide not-for-profit agency? Do we have a new business in town?

It's all investing. And, it's all beneficial for the community as a whole.

Do you know what that means? It means it's good for everyone…including me. Why? It gives me a sense of belonging, of pride, and of accomplishment to be a part of my community. And, that's great for my community's businesses as well as for my business."

Wendy VanHatten
Published Author, Magazine Editor, Travel Writer
www.wendyvanhatten.com
www.travelsandescapes.blogspot.com
amazon.com/author/wendyvanhatten
www.primetimeliving.org
http://wemagazineforwomen.com/
www.forkscorksandbrews.com

Anna J. Campbell

Investing In Your Community: Questions

1. What type of donations have you given to a community organization, fundraiser, or business function in the past year (items, gift certificates, etc.)? Always include your best products to represent you in the most attractive and appealing light.

_____

_____

2. Have the donation recipients ever contacted you about your services or products after winning? Have you noticed a difference in response depending on the event type or event organizer?

_____

3. Did the organization provide you with the winner's information?

_____

4. List out upcoming events you are interested in providing a donation for (list event name, date, deadline to submit, and what you want to donate):

_____

_____

_____

_____

5. What do you receive for donating items to the above events?

- ☐ Do you receive media exposure online or offline through advertising, press releases, articles?
- ☐ Do you have your business name acknowledged in an event program?
- ☐ Do you have your business name announced during the event?
- ☐ Do you receive a list of attendees for the event?
- ☐ Do you receive information about the person who won your donation?

6. Have you taken time to learn about other businesses in your market area?

7. Have you taken time to get to know other business leaders within your community?

8. How many other businesses have you told someone about?

9. Have you been highlighting other businesses that are complimentary to you in your monthly newsletter?

Investing In Your Community: Solutions

1. When donating an item, make sure the packaging is top of the line. Often that is what gets peoples' attention first.

2. Instead of including all full size products in your give-away use a large variety of sample sizes instead. This gives the basket a sense of variety and provides the winner with a wide range of options that you provide, and the incentive to visit you sooner because their favorite samples are used up faster!

3. Limit the number of donations per month, quarter or year.

4. Limit the total dollar amounts of donations per month, quarter or year.

5. Limit who and where you donate to, by identifying if they will be attracting your target market or not. You only want to provide donations to events or causes that will also attract people who would be interested in your products or services or because it benefits a cause close to your heart.

6. If you must provide a donation for an event or cause that does not attract your target market use your time wisely by purchasing a token gift that compliments the event and still brings good attention to you and your business name.

7. Saying no to additional donation requests is ok! It is good business sense. In fact, tell them you love supporting your local community, unfortunately you have already reached your donation budget limit at that time!

8. Always use donations as an opportunity to help spread the word about the event it is for, letting people know why you are supporting this event and how they also can attend or support the same event.

9. Be mindful to include information on your website, newsletter and online social media about organizations and charities you support.

Business Accountability: Tracking Goals from last month

Number of new clients added to your database: _____

Number of transactions/sales closed: _____

Number of networking events attended: _____

Number of referrals given: _____

Number of marketing pieces delivered: _____

Goals to accomplish this month

Number of new clients to add to my client list: _____

Number of transactions/sales to complete: _____

Number of networking events to attend: _____

Number of referrals to give others: _____

Number of marketing pieces to hand out or mail: _____

Chapter 10

Staying Sane By Forming a Power Group

FORMING A POWER GROUP WILL HELP YOU MAINTAIN
YOUR SANITY.

*"Never doubt that a small group of thoughtful committed citizens
can change the world; indeed it's the only thing that ever has."*
Margaret Mead

As a business leader you will often face challenges that your
family and friends do not understand and are not able to help you
deal with.

Forming a small group of fellow business leaders that are positive
and productive will provide you with a safe place to air your
concerns, doubts, questions, and accomplishments!

This group will help you stay accountable to your goals and will
help you stay encouraged and focused on your path. Each business
leader is unique and brings a fresh perspective and outlook on
different situations. Each business may also be at different stages

of developing their business. Including people who are unique and are at different phases of their business are keys for you to use when building a small and intimate group of people you can trust.

Knowing that you can be completely honest will give you a sense of security. Learning from your mistakes and the mistakes of others helps to make your journey more worthwhile and meaningful.

My friend Naomi Riley is a well-known and loved community leader in her home town. She has been forging the way for our community to embrace the arts, community life, and a productive downtown. During all of that time, while she has been committed to helping and serving so many others, she has also been building a strong and resilient group of enthusiasts and leaders around her.

I asked Naomi what her thoughts were about forming a Power Group and how it has helped her as the leader in her business and community.

"I believe in the power of conversation and accountability. With my small "accountability" group I work with other small business owners as we explore ideas together. We each leave with three things we must accomplish before the next meeting.

In business success I feel having this kind of support is what helps you stay focused and goal oriented. Plus, it's fun to get together with others who are living the American Dream!

I love my group!"

Naomi Riley
The Polished Table
http://thepolishedtable.com
www.facebook.com/pages/The-Polished-Table/322705221232387

Staying Sane: Questions

1. Consider local business and community leaders within your community:

- Who do you consider to be your role model within your local area?

_____

- Who would you most benefit from being around and learning from within your local area?

_____

_____

- Who would provide you with access to skills, tools, or contacts that would help you be a better business leader from within your local area?

_____

_____

2. Taking a moment to consider the people on your list of potential Power Group members:

- Who would also benefit from being in this group from you?

_____

- What do you have to offer to each of the people on your list?

_____

- How would this prove to be worth their time and effort? What topics would you discuss? What will be your focus areas? How much time will be person have during the meeting?

_____

_____

- Do these people already belong to a "Power Group"?

Staying Sane: Solutions

1. The perfect Power Group includes:
   - Focus on mutual benefit
   - 3-5 people only
   - Not referral focused
   - Growth and sustainability focused
   - Usually held monthly for 1 hour

2. Don't just focus on yourself:
   - Include each of them in your regular thinking process
   - Build strong bonds on trust and accountability

3. It is best to only belong to one Power Group. Sharing your intimate worries should remain with a small trustworthy group of people.

4. This should be a very positive group with no guilt or accusations. True accountability with purpose.

Business Accountability: Tracking Goals from last month

Number of new clients added to your database: _____

Number of transactions/sales closed: _____

Number of networking events attended: _____

Number of referrals given: _____

Number of marketing pieces delivered: _____

Goals to accomplish this month

Number of new clients to add to my client list: _____

Number of transactions/sales to complete: _____

Number of networking events to attend: _____

Number of referrals to give others: _____

Number of marketing pieces to hand out or mail: _____

Anna J. Campbell

Chapter 11

Celebrating Your Successes

THIS CONCEPT MAY SEEM SIMPLE OR EVEN TRIFLE TO MANY BUSINESS LEADERS WHO ARE BUSY SELECTING THEIR NEXT SEASONAL PRODUCT LINE OR SETTING-UP THEIR UPCOMING SPEAKING SERIES.

"Learning to celebrate success is a key component of learning how to win in the market." Douglas Conant

However, by completing this simple and very calming practice, you can actually boost your sales and productivity.

Each morning prior to starting your "business day" take a few minutes and think about what positive and productive things have been happening within your business over the past few days and weeks.

Evaluate your current sales against your sales during the same time period last year.

Look back at website articles or facebook posts from last year and see how much you have accomplished and grown.

Think about the products or services you were offering last year at this time and look at your current product or service line. Do you see improvements in quality? Do you see a more focused and attentive theme?

Sometimes we are so busy moving forward, we forget to appreciate how far we have actually come.

As we evaluate our business success, we need to remember all of the people who helped us accomplish our goals and succeed with our plans. Some of the people who helped you may include: customers, fellow business leaders, business organizations, networking groups, mentors, coaches, friends, family, and possibly your own competitors.

Remember to vocally and visibly thank everyone who has helped you accomplish each of your successes!

A few ways I have shown my appreciation in the past has included: sending thank you cards, dropping off gifts to my best clients, and posting appreciation comments on my social media to a specific group of clients, mentors, friends, or fellow business leaders.

One of the easiest and most rewarding techniques I have used was sending an old fashioned thank you card. This seemed to garner more appreciation and admiration from the recipients, even more than the pricey gifts or public announcements I made for or about them. This simple act of kindness really helped brighten their day and reminded them how very important and special they were to me and my business.

I did not use a thank you card as a way to solicit more business. If I did not know them personally as a friend, I would include my business card so they could easily get in touch with me, but I never included a coupon, or incentive to purchase any of my services or products.

A business owner here in my local community, Kim Draper who owns KnB's Marketplace, has really impressed me with her ingenious way of showing gratitude for her vendors who supply the majority of the unique and exciting products in her store. Kim hosts an appreciation night for her vendors where she encourages them to have fun and take some time to get to know the other vendors.

This event gives her the opportunity to thank each of them for all of their hard work with their individual businesses and support for each other.

Kim Draper
KnB's Marketplace
120 Raleigh St., Fuquay-Varina, NC 27526
www.facebook.com/pages/KnBS-Marketplace/297793476917848
(919) 557-8155

I wish you congratulations on your successes and congratulations on your growth! May this year prove to be even more rewarding for you and your business!

Celebrating Your Successes: Questions

1. Who should be included in your celebration?

_____

_____

2. Who has helped you accomplish your goals? You are not an island. Include employees, friends, customers, other business leaders, people who refer business to you, etc.

_____

_____

_____

_____

3. How do you most enjoy celebrating?
- Big parties
- Intimate dinners
- Short get-away
- A day off to read or work in your garden
- Showering others with gifts
- Taking out ad space in your local newspaper or magazine with a celebration notice

_____

_____

_____

_____

Celebrating Your Successes: Solutions

1. Your focus here is to celebrate in small ways every day, every week, and in big ways every year.

2. Your goal is to embrace those who have helped you, thanking them encourages them to continue helping you. It will also encourage those around you, who may not have helped you so far, feel more inclined to be more supportive in the future.

3. This practice will raise moral for you and everyone else involved.

Business Accountability: Tracking Goals from last month

Number of new clients added to your database: _____

Number of transactions/sales closed: _____

Number of networking events attended: _____

Number of referrals given: _____

Number of marketing pieces delivered: _____

Goals to accomplish this month

Number of new clients to add to my client list: _____

Number of transactions/sales to complete: _____

Number of networking events to attend: _____

Number of referrals to give others: _____

Number of marketing pieces to hand out or mail: _____

Chapter 12

Business Resources

YOUR BUSINESS RESOURCES WILL BE THE TOOLS YOU USE TO CONDUCT AND GROW YOUR BUSINESS.

In this chapter I will share many business resources that have proven useful to save time, money, and have helped business leaders be more productive.

Wordpress: https://wordpress.com/

- Fairly easy user-friendly platform for building websites using premade templates. This platform can be free through wordpress.com or you can purchase hosting and utilize the plethora of options from wordpress.org.

Google Calendar: https://www.google.com/calendar/

- Stay in the loop with upcoming internal business meetings, external fun outings, and personal itineraries. This can be set-up for groups or individuals. Calendars can be posted privately or publicly on websites and online platforms.

Online Social Media:

- Twitter: https://twitter.com/
  - Way to promote products and services through short written posts with or without pictures in a primarily business resource
- Pinterest: https://www.pinterest.com/
  - Way to promote products and services through pictures in a primarily non-business resource
- LinkedIn: https://www.linkedin.com/
  - Way to promote your experiences, skills and education in a primarily business resource
- Facebook: https://www.facebook.com/
  - Way to promote your business news, products, and services in a primarily non-business resource

Intuit Mint: https://www.mint.com/

- From money and budgeting to customized tips and more – get a clear view of your total financial life.

Survey Monkey: https://www.surveymonkey.com

- SurveyMonkey says they are the world's most popular online survey software. They make it easier than ever to create polls and survey questionnaires for learning about anything from customer satisfaction to employee engagement.
- Sign up to access their library of sample survey questions and expert-certified templates. Customize your survey questions, distribute your questionnaire on the web, and start collecting responses in real time. Their Analyze tool helps you turn survey data into insights and create professional reports.

Jennifer Vaaler with Transpire Life shared two of her most useful programs and products with us:

Evernote

- I used to have a hard time shutting my brain off to get sleep. I started using Evernote as a "brain dump" of ideas, lists, and research into one place. It turned all my brain chaos into an organized, easy to find system.
- You can set up notebooks and sub folders by project. Then, as you add notes and research, you simply use a chrome extension to save something into the main topic folder then 'tag' (like keywords) for other sub topics. So when you search for a specific keyword, it'll pull up anything saved under that keyword.
- This has saved me hours of setting up blog posts, adding references to articles etc, and I get more sleep because I know my ideas will be in Evernote to look back over in the morning.

My Planner

- I carry my Planner everywhere. I have a binder for each project and business that I leave at home so my Planner is an overview of all my projects, business and life in one place.
- I'm a very visual person, and use google calendar, but I must write things down into my planner to help me remember better.
- I set up my Planner to suit my lifestyle, not the other way around, so I'm most likely to use it effectively. I couldn't really find a Planner that met my needs so I found one that I can customize and easily move things around to adapt to a new routine. Accessories for my Planner brighten it up yet leave the black and white pages for easy reading and focus on what needs done. And if it's not in my planner, it won't get done.

Between just these two tools, I stay on track and get everything knocked out that needs accomplished each day.

Jennifer Vaaler

Transpire Life

http://transpirelife.com/

https://www.facebook.com/TranspireLife

Anna J. Campbell

Business Plan Template

Here are things to include in your business plan.

(update every 6 to 12 months)

Business Name:

- Established Date:
- Business Type (Sole Proprietorship, LLC, etc):
- Business License file date:
- EIN:
- Sales Tax License file date:

Insurance Coverage Company:

- Insurance Company Phone Number:
- Renewal Date:
- Coverage Amount:

CPA Company Name:

- CPA Contact Name:
- CPA Phone Number:
- CPA Email Address:

Attorney Company Name:

- Attorney Contact Name:
- Attorney Phone Number:
- Attorney Email Address:

Desired Annual Revenue:

- Actual Annual Revenue 1st Year:
- Actual Annual Revenue 3rd Year:
- Actual Annual Revenue 5th Year:
- Actual Annual Revenue 10th Year:

Products/Services:

- List products or services for sale:
- List average price of products or services:
- Date of last product/service review:

Customers:

- Date of last customer survey:
- Number of desired new clients per month:
- Client database (current number of clients):

Online:

- Website URL:
    - Website Domain Company URL:
    - Website Hosting Company URL:
    - Website Developer Company Name:
    - Website Developer Email:
    - Website Developer Phone Number:
    - Date of last website update:
- Facebook URL:
- Twitter URL:
- LinkedIn URL:

Offline:

- Local Media Contact Name:
- Local Media Contact Email:
- Local Media Contact Phone Number:
- Date of last marketing campaign:

Number of Employees:

- What type of benefits do you provide for your Employees:

Professional or Civic Groups you belong to:

Awards or Accomplishments you and your business have received:

REFERENCES

Alyssa Mattero a contributing author with Shareaholic

Beth Glover owner of Merle Norman

Bobbie Asad owner of Mad Hatter

Brenda Lagnese owner of Furry Friends of Fuquay

Cindy Clark owner of CC Transformational Coaching

Claire Shipman and Katty Kay authors of womenomics

Ekaterina Walter a contributing writer with Forbes

Gretchen Rubin author of The Happiness Project

Heidi Cohen with Actionable Marketing Guide

Jennifer Vaaler owner of Transpire Life

JJ Ramberg author of It's Your Business

Julie Bell Voorhees owner of Bumblebee Market

Kim Draper owner of KnB's Marketplace

Liz Papagni a contributing writer with Business 2 Community

Lou Ibriano, CEO of TrinityOne, a contributing author with American Express

Martha Stewart author of The Martha Rules

Naomi Riley owner of The Polished Table

Sara Germano and Anna Prior contributing writers with the Wall Street Journal

Wendy VanHatten published author, magazine editor, and travel writer

DISCLAIMER

Please take note that there is no quick or overnight way to create a strong and thriving business. To be a strong business leader, one needs to build their skills, knowledge, and expertise over time.

Summaries, strategies, and tips are only recommendations by the author, and reading this book does not guarantee that one's results will exactly mirror her results. The author of 12 Healthy Habits of Business Leadership has made all reasonable efforts to provide current and accurate information for the readers of this book. The author will not be held liable for any unintentional errors or omissions that may be found.

ABOUT THE AUTHOR

Anna J. Campbell loves being involved with organizations and businesses that actively provide services on a local, national and international level.

Her focus areas include: business marketing research, business marketing counseling, networking, women empowerment, and gender violation issues.

Anna and her family enjoy the historical charms of their late Queen Anne style home that was built in 1910.
Ballentine-Spence House
www.BallentineSpenceHouse.com

Anna provides additional resources and tools on her website:
www.MrsAnnaCampbell.com

www.ingramcontent.com/pod-product-compliance
Lightning Source LLC
Chambersburg PA
CBHW070903180526
45168CB00005B/1916